Friendshi
Famous Quotes,
and a Journal

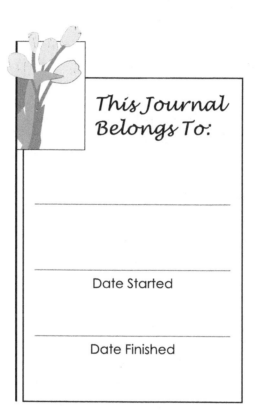

This Journal
Belongs To:

_____

_____

Date Started

_____

Date Finished

Hannacroix Creek Books, Inc.
Stamford, Connecticut

Friendship Thoughts, Famous Quotes, and a Journal

Introduction, selections, contact directory, resources, and bibliography, copyright © 2014 by Jan Yager

Published by:
Hannacroix Creek Books, Inc.
1127 High Ridge Road, #110
Stamford, Connecticut 06905 USA
hannacroix@aol.com
www.hannacroixcreekbooks.com
Follow us on twitter: www.twitter.com/hannacroixcreek

ISBN: 978-1-938998-79-9 (hardcover)
ISBN: 978-1-938998-80-5 (trade paperback)

Friendship Thoughts

Whether you are sixty-five or five, having friends means a lot to all of us. As today we celebrate friendship, throughout history friendship has also been the subject of philosophers, poets, essayists, authors, playwrights, and filmmakers, as well as sociologists, psychologists, celebrities, and just plain folk with insights to share. The selected quotes about friendship in this journal is a testament to those inspirational perspectives on friendship over time.

Besides my own experiences growing up, beginning with my close friendship with Ginny, who lived next door in Bayside, Queens, New York, my first awareness as a researcher of the power of friendship began when I was conducting interviews for my book, *Single in America*. In carrying out that research, I discovered that those singles who had a strong network of friends, or even one close or best friend, even if unattached to a romantic partner, tended to be more content with their lives; they were not lonely. Their friends were their glue. The power of friendship was confirmed in the interviews I later conducted for my sociology dissertation on friendship, as well as the additional primary and secondary research I have done over the next decades on this fascinating topic.

This journal, in addition to its usefulness as a journal, is a celebration of friendship that includes 140 quotes about friendship, including several short poems, that I've been collecting for decades from a variety of published and online sources including from five of my own books on friendship and relationships including *Friendshifts; When Friendship Hurts; 365 Daily Affirmations for Friendship; Who's That Sitting at My Desk? Workship, Friendship, or Foe*; and *Productive Relationships*.

Although, as so many have noted, making friends is the "work" of the childhood, teen, and young adult years, we all know that making friends actually has little to do with age. There are ample opportunities to form friendships as we age if we allow ourselves to be open to it, emotionally and in terms of making time for others. This was brought home to me in a very concrete way soon after my book *Friendshifts* was published. I was giving a lecture about the value of friendship to seniors. During the question and answer session, a woman who looked to be in her

80s — I soon learned she was actually in her 90s— raised her hand. She explained she was widowed and that all her friends had died. She did not have any friends anymore.

I took a deep breath and without being judgmental or critical, I shared with her that perhaps it was time for her to make new friends. And that the wonderful thing about friendship is that you can make a new friend, at any time and at any age.

Whether you are 95, 55, 63, 22, or 18, whether you are single and unattached, married, or anything in-between, positive friendships can make an amazing difference in the quality of our lives and even in how long we live. Research has confirmed that friendship is a factor in longevity, adding as much as ten years. It also helps to have a friend to prevent getting sick in the first place or if you have cancer or a heart attack, friendship is a factor in how quickly you recover.

Technology is changing friendship for so many of us as keeping up with our friends' activities through social media is more common now. Of course there are still those who have never used a computer. For them, the phone, letters, or getting together in person are their traditional ways to stay connected. By contrast, my 88-year-old mother-in-law recently asked me to "friend her" on Facebook.com.

Everyone accepts that there is love at first sight. The same thing can happen with friendship. You can take an instant like or even a dislike to someone that you meet. But just like with love, it is key to figure out, as you get to know someone, if your initial impressions are matched by what you learn is your new acquaintance's true character. Will this "fast friend" become a tried-and-true friend? (My research found that it took, on average, three years from meeting to becoming tried-and-true friends who had passed the "tests" on the friendship along the way.)

Here is a summary of some of the other findings from my friendship research that you might find useful to consider:

- Shared values are the best predictor of longevity in a friendship; finding out what someone is at their core is key.
- Ideally you can tell your friends anything you want to share but you also have the right to decide what you will share and with whom.

- Yes, birds of a feather do flock together but opposites also attract.
- Cut your friends some slack if they're going through a tough time or if they are really busy with work or family obligations.
- Be especially kind to your longstanding friends because you can't ever replace those memories, years, or relationships even if you do form newer friendships.
- It's not whether or not you have any conflicts that indicate if a friendship will, or should, continue, it is how you handle your conflicts.
- There is a myth that "true friendship" is smooth. That is as unrealistic as assuming true love is devoid of conflict.
- Betrayal can mean not being there for someone emotionally so be careful what you promise: promise less, deliver more.
- Don't ask your friends to choose between your friendship and their romantic or familial relationships because you know who will most likely come up short.
- Emotional support and shared activities count but always remember to keep — or put — the fun factor into your friendships.
- Children learn more from your example than they do from words so if you want them to have excellent friendship skills, remember to make time for your own friends, no matter how busy you might be.
- Be a good and reliable friend to your friends.
- Remember your friends' birthdays; get together in person but if that's not possible, use social media, e-mail, send a text message, or, even better, call on the phone. Send a card or exchange token gifts, if you both agree to that tradition.
- Communicate regularly with your friend, just to say hello and not just to share good or sad news.
- There may be averages of how many friends are typical in each of the categories of best, close, or casual —1-2 best, 4-6 close, and 10-20 casual — but remember that you can have as many friends as you can handle.
- There's a new category of friends that I call FBF — Facebook Friends. These friendships may be in the

casual category, or they may be closer to what I call a workship, if it's a work-related FBF, more than an acquaintance but less than a traditional friend. These FBFs count, even if they are "just" FBF as evidenced by the outpouring of birthday greetings you may get from your FBF, even if, in the past, you just got one or two cards from your traditional friendship network.

- Friendship at work can be complicated especially if it's between those who are unequal in status, e.g. a boss and an employee. But friendship between co-workers, and even between those unequal in status if you are careful to avoid anything that smacks of favoritism, can make your job and workplace much more joyful and productive.

On Keeping a Journal

I started keeping a journal when I was just ten years old; I still keep one today. When I reread my first journal, which I sometimes do, on occasion, it's a way of reconnecting with the person I used to be. It is very different than remembering people or experiences from where I am now. I have discovered that a journal is a gift we give ourselves by sharing our thoughts, experiences, feelings, and observations at one specific point in time. We might just write those thoughts down only for ourselves, or we might want to share those thoughts with others, right away, months, years, or even decades later.

I have also found that keeping a journal or diary has been a catharsis for me as I commit to paper in a detailed way what I was thinking and feeling. I even use a journal for taking notes when I attend a conference, or as a way to keep track of ideas that I want to explore, although I may also write down comments on my smart phone or computer. For me, keeping a journal has evolved into keeping everything in one convenient place, not just a reflection on my feelings but also a way of taking notes. I even recently used removable adhesive "note tabs" that are for indexing, as a way of better organizing the notes in a journal by putting the tabs in key places.

As the article, "Journaling for Mental Health," published at the website for the University of Rochester Medical Center points out, journaling can aid your mental state by helping you to "manage stress, reduce stress, and cope with depression."

Writing in a journal has led to a published book in countless instances, including the cherished *Anne Frank: The Diary of A Young Girl*, published posthumously in 1947, which was the diary that 13-year-old Anne kept during the two years that she hid out from the Nazis in Amsterdam before her eventual death in a concentration camp.

When and why someone writes in a journal is an individual decision. As Irene and Alan Taylor point out in their introduction to the 710-page collection, *The Assassin's Cloak: An Anthology of the World's Greatest Diarists*, "Some diarists, such as Walter Scott, write during times of emotional and financial crisis, others when they are at their most happy and socially active."

Deborah Chenault Green's sister-in-law gave her a journal as a way of dealing with her youngest brother's death in 2002. Although Deborah initially put the journal aside, as she explains: "I later picked the journal up and my emotions started pouring out onto the pages." Then, in 2008, she published her journal in book form: *Back 2/1: I Invite You Into My Serenity: A Collection of Poetry and Prose*. Deborah continues about the many advantages of journaling: "The benefits of journaling have been proven in my life and have stretched far beyond writing. I have since become an actress and director, also things I had never done before, or aspired to before."

So Why a Friendship Journal?

Throughout *Friendship Thoughts, Famous Quotes, and A Journal*, you will discover 140 friendship quotes from famous philosophers, authors, celebrities, poets, friendship researchers, and other sources. Some of the quotes you may already have read elsewhere, since these are the words of the classical "great" friendship thinkers, like Cicero, Aristotle, Montaigne, Emerson, Thoreau, Dorothy Parker, and Dale Carnegie. Other quotes may be new to you, offering you delightful surprises, like the quote about loving and befriending yourself from the nonfiction mega-bestseller *How to Be Your Own Best Friend*, that begins this journal. Or a quote from the classic contemporary bestseller *Never Eat Alone* by Keith Ferrazzi with Tahl Raz.

After those journal pages, with each journal page having a friendship quote at the top, there are four additional journal pages where you can write down your own original friendship quotes or any additional sayings that you discover. After that, there are two blank unlined pages where you can draw or doodle or even add photos of you and your friends.

Following the journaling part of this book, I have reprinted a self-quiz to help you assess your current friendships, a list of several ways to make time for your friends, excerpted from *Friendshifts*, and a checklist for a positive friendship, excerpted from *When Friendship Hurts*, and, finally, "The Friendship Oath" that I created, originally published in *Who's That Sitting at My Desk?*

Also included in this unique journal is an e-mail and telephone/cell phone directory where you may record key contact information to make it easier to stay in communication with your friends.

Finally, this journal concludes with a resource section of some useful friendship sites and a selected bibliography on this amazing relationship we call friendship.

You can, of course, use this journal solely as a way to explore the topic of friendship as well as your own friendship concerns from celebrating the joys of a new or evolving friendship to helping you to heal from a friendship that has ended. Or you can use this journal to explore anything and everything you want to write about.

Remember that friendship is not just an "extra" in our lives. We need friends. As poet John Dunne wrote centuries ago, "No man is an island," and that's as true now as it was back then, when you had to write letters or visit in person to stay in touch.

But I want to conclude this introduction with a plea that you, my dear reader and journal keeper, remember that, first and foremost, the most pivotal friendship is the one you have with yourself. I celebrate you, first and foremost! You are a wonderful person worthy of befriending yourself as well as others.

Appreciate yourself in all your uniqueness because you are most definitely deserving of self-love. Friendship with others are, of course, wonderful to have as well but friendships can end for so many reasons, from the passing away of a friend to a friend moving away to a falling out that, even if temporarily, puts the friendship on hold.

The best defense against the potentially devastating consequences of bullying or even of being rejected by a friend or group of friends is having that primary friendship with yourself. That is relationship that will spur you on so you can deal with the bullying, repair the friendship, or find new, more positive friendships.

So, dear reader and journal keeper, happy reading and writing in this journal. I hope you enjoy reading, and writing in, *Friendship Thoughts, Famous Quotes, and a Journal* as much as I've appreciated compiling these quotes and creating it.

I welcome hearing from you about your favorite quotes, your own friendships, or how writing in this journal is useful and enjoyable to you.

Decades in preparation, I welcome the publication of this journal as a catalyst to a continuing global dialogue about friendship.

Happy reading! Rewarding writing!

Jan Yager, Ph.D.
drjanyager.com
whenfriendshiphurts.com

Follow me on Twitter:
http://www.twitter.com/drjanyager

"We can learn to be our own best friend. If we do, we have a friend for life."

—Mildred Newman and Bernard Berkowitz (psychologists) with Jean Owen (writer), *How to Be Your Own Best Friend* (1971)

_____

_____

_____

_____

_____

_____

_____

_____

_____

_____

_____

_____

_____

_____

_____

_____

_____

_____

_____

_____

_____

_____

_____

_____

_____

_____

"Don't walk in front of me,
I may not follow.
Don't walk behind me, I may
not lead.
Walk beside me,
And just be my friend."

—Albert Camus

_____

_____

_____

_____

_____

_____

_____

_____

_____

_____

_____

_____

_____

_____

_____

_____

_____

_____

_____

_____

_____

_____

_____

_____

_____

_____

"The holy passion of Friendship is of so sweet and steady and loyal and enduring a nature that it will last through a whole lifetime, if not asked to lend money."

—Mark Twain, *Pudd'nhead Wilson*, 1894

"'They're my friends.'
'I am very well aware of that.
Why do you choose such
odd friends?'
'One doesn't choose friends.
One acquires them. They are
as much duty as pleasure.'"
—Fay Weldon, novelist, *Female Friends* (1974)

"What could be finer than to have someone to whom you may speak as freely as to yourself? How could you derive true joy from good fortune, if you did not have someone who would rejoice in your happiness as much as you yourself? And it would be very hard to bear misfortune in the absence of anyone who would take your sufferings even harder than you."

—Cicero, *"On Friendship,"* translated by Frank O. Copley

> *"Happiness is a by-product of an effort to make someone else happy."*
> —journalist Gretta Palmer

_____

_____

_____

_____

_____

_____

_____

_____

_____

_____

_____

_____

_____

_____

_____

_____

_____

_____

_____

_____

_____

_____

_____

_____

_____

_____

_____

_____

"I was angry with my friend;
I told my wrath, my wrath
did end.
I was angry with my foe;
I told it not, my wrath
did grow."

—William Blake, (1757-1827), poet, "A
Poison Tree"

_____

_____

_____

_____

_____

_____

_____

_____

_____

_____

_____

_____

_____

_____

_____

_____

_____

_____

_____

_____

_____

_____

_____

_____

_____

_____

"People who instinctively establish a strong network of relationships have always greatest great businesses. If you strip business down to its basics, it's still about people selling things to other people."

—Keith Ferrazzi with Tahl Raz, *Never Eat Alone*

"If you are willing to strike up a conversation, you could meet someone in line at the post office, ordering a Decaf Java Chip Frappucini at Starbucks, or scoping the decorations at an office Christmas party. Almost any spot has friend-making potential."

—Roger Horchow and Sally Horchow, *The Art of Friendship*

"To me, friendship is as simple as seeking comfort or companionship from another to improve one's own life experience."

—Jennifer Holland, *Unlikely Friendships: 47 Remarkable Stories from the Animal Kingdom*

"In the friendship I speak of, our souls mingle and blend with each other so completely that they efface the seam that joined them, and cannot find it again."

—Montaigne, *"Of Friendship,"* translated by Donald Frame

"Friendship consists in forgetting what one gives and remembering what one receives."

—Alexandre Dumas (1802-1870), French writer

_____
_____
_____
_____
_____
_____
_____
_____
_____
_____
_____
_____
_____
_____
_____
_____
_____
_____
_____
_____
_____
_____
_____
_____
_____
_____
_____
_____
_____

"Every murderer is probably somebody's old friend."

—Agatha Christie (1890-1976), British crime novelist, *The Mysterious Affair at Styles* (1920)

"In research at our clinic, my colleagues and I have discovered that friendship is the springboard to the other important relationships of life. "

—psychotherapist Alan Loy McGinnis, *The Friendship Factor*

"*All people have their fancies; some desire horses, and others dogs; and some are fond of gold, and others of honor. Now, I have no violent desire of any of these things; but I have a passion for friends; and I would rather have a good friend than the best cock or quail in the world: I would even go further, and say the best horse or dog...*"

—Plato, *Lysis, or Friendship*

_____

_____

_____

_____

_____

_____

_____

_____

_____

_____

_____

_____

_____

_____

_____

_____

_____

_____

_____

_____

_____

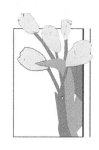

"*Personally, I think that Aristotle is on to something in his belief that the closest kind of friendship is only possible with one or two individuals, such is the investment of time and self that it takes.*"

—Mark Vernon, *The Philosophy of Friendship*

"Outside of family, the women I'm closest to are the ones I went to college with. We skipped classes together, scrambled eggs in the middle of the night, know each other inside and out."

—former talk show host and author Jane Pauley, quoted in Zivs Kwitney's article, "Bosom Buddies," in the *Seattle Post-Intelligencer* (2/15/81)

"It is hard to say, 'I need friends.'"

—Shasta Nelson, *Friendships Don't Just Happen!*

_____

_____

_____

_____

_____

_____

_____

_____

_____

_____

_____

_____

_____

_____

_____

_____

_____

_____

_____

_____

_____

_____

_____

_____

_____

_____

_____

_____

_____

_____

_____

"*It is easy enough to be friendly to one's friends. But to befriend the one who regards himself as your enemy is the quintessence of true religion. The other is mere business.*"

—Mohandas K. Gandhi, *Non-Violence in Peace and War*, vol. 2 (1948)

> *"We see things not as they are, but as we are."*
> —H. M. Tomlinson

_____

_____

_____

_____

_____

_____

_____

_____

_____

_____

_____

_____

_____

_____

_____

_____

_____

_____

_____

_____

_____

_____

_____

_____

_____

_____

_____

_____

"By accepting the responsibility of friendship, I promise to be honest and trustworthy. I will try to work out any conflicts that we may have and will try to put the time and effort into our friendship that it requires."

—Jan Yager, excerpted from "Friendship Oath," in *Who's That Sitting at My Desk? Workship, Friendship, or Foe?*

"Who ceases to be a friend never was one."
—Greek proverb

_____

_____

_____

_____

_____

_____

_____

_____

_____

_____

_____

_____

_____

_____

_____

_____

_____

_____

_____

_____

_____

_____

_____

_____

_____

_____

_____

_____

_____

"Rather than urging your loved ones to conform, encourage their uniqueness. Everyone has dreams, dreams that no one else has, and you can make yourself loved by encouraging those aspirations."

—Alan Joy McGinnis, Ph.D., *The Friendship Factor* (2004; 1979)

"It has been held that friendship is actually immoral in that it entails giving preferential treatment to people who may neither need nor deserve it more than others."

—D.J. Enright and David Rawlinson, editors, *The Oxford Book of Friendship*

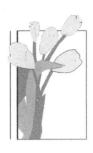

"Friendship arises out of mere Companionship when two or more of the companions discover that they have in common some insight or interest or even taste which the others do not share and which, till that moment, each believed to be his own unique treasure (or burden). The typical expression of opening Friendship would be something like, 'What? You too? I thought I was the only one.'"
—C.S. Lewis, "Friendship—The Least Necessary Love." Quoted in *Friendship: A Philosophical Reader.* Edited by Neera Kapur Badhwar

> *"The people in one's life are like the pillars on one's porch you see life through. And sometimes they hold you up, and sometimes they lean on you, and sometimes it's just enough to know they're standing by."*
>
> —Merle Shain, *When Lovers are Friends*

"Friendship is a pretty full-time occupation if you really are friendly with somebody. You can't have too many friends because then you're just not really friends."

—Truman Capote, author, *Conversations with Truman Capote*, edited by Lawrence Grobel, 1985

> *"He [my father] taught me: keep your friends close, but your enemies closer."*
> —Michael Corleone, *The Godfather, Part II*, screenplay by Francis Ford Coppolla and Mario Puzo

_____

_____

_____

_____

_____

_____

_____

_____

_____

_____

_____

_____

_____

_____

_____

_____

_____

_____

_____

_____

_____

_____

_____

_____

_____

"He makes no friend who never made a foe."

—Tennyson, *"Lancelot and Elaine,"* 1859

"A friend may well be reckoned the masterpiece of nature."
—Ralph Waldo Emerson,
"Friendship," Essays

"Knowledge is what you learn from others; wisdom is what you teach yourself."
—Unknown

"The mere process of growing old together will make the slightest acquaintance seem a bosom friend."

—Logan Pearsall Smith, U.S. essayist, *All Trivia* (1933)

"Make new friends but keep the old; one is silver, but the other is gold."

—Girl Scouts song

> "...A man cannot speak to his son but as a father; to his wife but as a husband; to his enemy but upon terms; whereas a friend may speak as the case requires, and not as it sorteth with the person."

—Sir Francis Bacon, "Of friendship," *The Essays, or Counsels, Civil and Moral*, 1625

"There is a curious fact about friendship that we have always known but rarely acknowledge: By understanding others, we also come closer to understanding ourselves."
—Bradley Trevor Greive,
Friends to the End

"Reprove a friend in secret but praise him before others."
—Leonardo de Vinci, *Notebooks*

_____

_____

_____

_____

_____

_____

_____

_____

_____

_____

_____

_____

_____

_____

_____

_____

_____

_____

_____

_____

_____

_____

_____

_____

_____

_____

_____

_____

_____

_____

_____

_____

"When trouble comes, do not go running to your brother's house. Better a friend near than a brother far away."

—The Proverbs of Solomon (27)

> *"Better a whole-hearted feud*
> *Than a friendship that*
> *is glued."*
> —Friedrich Nietzsche, German
> philosopher, *The Gay Science* (1881)

"The essence of friendship is entireness, a total magnanimity and trust."
—Ralph Waldo Emerson, essayist,
"Friendship" (1845)

"So the cardinal rule for every person who desires better relationships is 'Learn to zipper your lip.' Nothing causes people to clam up and to abandon your friendship more quickly than to discover that you have revealed a private matter."

—Alan Joy McGinnis, Ph.D., *The Friendship Factor (2004; 1979)*

"Equality is felt to be an essential element of friendship."

—Aristotle, Book VIII, *The Nicomachean Ethics*

"No receipt openeth the heart,
but a true friend to whom
you may impart griefs, joys,
fears, hopes, suspicions,
counsels, and whatsoever
lieth upon the heart to
oppress it, in a kind of civil
shrift or confession."

—Sir Francis Bacon, *The Essays, or
Counsels,* "Of Friendship" (1625)

_____

_____

_____

_____

_____

_____

_____

_____

_____

_____

_____

_____

_____

_____

_____

_____

_____

_____

_____

_____

_____

_____

_____

_____

"Do not desert an old friend;
the new one will not be
his match.
New friend, new wine;
when it grows old, you drink
it with pleasure."

—Ecclesiasticus

*"A constant friend is a thing
rare and hard to find."*
—Plutarch

"Friendships begin with liking or gratitude—roots that can be pulled up."

—George Eliot, novelist

> *"When it comes to friendship,*
> *quality counts more*
> *than quantity."*
> *(Affirmation #101)*
> —Jan Yager, *365 Daily Affirmations*
> *for Friendship*

_____
_____
_____
_____
_____
_____
_____
_____
_____
_____
_____
_____
_____
_____
_____
_____
_____
_____
_____
_____
_____
_____
_____
_____
_____
_____
_____
_____
_____

"'Friendship is Love without his wings!'"

—Lord Byron, poet

> *"Only solitary men know the full joys of friendship. Others have their family—but to a solitary and an exile his friends are everything."*
> —Willa Cather, novelist, *Shadows on the Rock* (1931)

"The good news is that while friendship may be a repetition of past familial relationships, it may also be an opportunity to work on, and even improve, those early interactions."

—Jan Yager, *Friendshifts*

"The most fatal disease of friendship is gradual decay, or dislike hourly increased by causes too slender for complaint, and too numerous for removal."
—Samuel Johnson

"Friendship can only exist between persons with similar interests and points of view. Man and woman by the conventions of society are born with different interests and different points of view."

—J. August Strindberg, Swedish playwright, *The Son of a Servant* (translated by Claud Field)

"*The three stages of the art of forgiving—restoring humanity to the person who wronged us, surrendering our right to get even, and beginning to bless the person we forgive—are the fundamentals of the healing process. No matter who did the wrong or who does the forgiving, when we forgive, we walk this pathway toward healing inside the wounded places of our own minds.*"

—Lewis B. Smedes, *The Art of Forgiving*

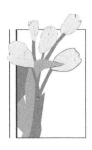

"The romanticized ideal that friendships should not end or fail may create unnecessary distress in those who should end a friendship but hold on, no matter what."

—Jan Yager, *When Friendship Hurts*

"Then we may say that the
greatest friendship is
of opposites?"
—Plato, *Lysis, or Friendship*

"Friendship is a virtue."

—Aristotle, *The Nicomachean Ethics*

"We praise those who love their friends, and it is counted a noble thing to have many friends; and some people think that a true friend must be a good man."

—Aristotle, *Nicomachean Ethics*, VIII, translated by H. Rackham

"Quarrel? Nonsense,; we have not quarreled. If one is not to get into a rage sometimes, what is the good of being friends?"

—George Eliot, novelist, *Middlemarch* (1871)

"'Men's friendships—oh yes! I know one hears a lot about them. But half the time, I don't believe they're real friendships at all. Men can go off for years and forget all about their friends. And they don't really confide in one another. Mary and I tell each other all our thoughts and feelings. Men seem just content to tell each other good sorts without ever bothering about their inmost selves.'

'Probably, that's why their friendships last so well,' replied Miss Climpson. 'They don't make such demands on one another.'"

—Dorothy L. Sayers, novelist,
Unnatural Death, 1927

"To be loved, be lovable."

—Ovid (43 B.C.-A.D. c. 18),

Ars Amatoria, II

"You can make more friends in two months by becoming really interested in other people, than you can in two years by trying to get other people interested in you. Which is just another way of saying that the way to make a friend is to be one."

—Dale Carnegie, *How to Win Friends and Influence People*

"It is one of the blessings of old friends that you can afford to be stupid with them."

—Ralph Waldo Emerson, *Journals* (1836)

"There are no strangers, only friends we haven't met."
—Anonymous

"Laughter is not at all a bad beginning for a friendship, and it is far the best ending for one."
—Oscar Wilde, *The Picture of Dorian Gray* (1891)

"What men have called friendship is only a social arrangement, a mutual adjustment of interests, an interchange of services given and received; it is, in sum, simply a business from which those involved propose to derive a steady profit for their own self-love."

—Francois, Duc de la Rouchefoucauld, French author, *Sentences et Maximes Morales* (1678)

"A good friend informs you ever so discreetly when you have spinach stuck between your teeth."

—Joseph Cohen (*Good Friend*)

"All of my friends understand my needs. I have many friends who love me."
—Louise L. Hay, #339, *Power Thoughts: 365 Daily Affirmations*

"There are two elements that go to the composition of friendship...One is Truth... The other element of friendship is tenderness."

—Ralph Waldo Emerson, "Friendship," *Essays (1841)*

> *"A single dominant friendship dissolves all other obligations."*
> —Montaigne, French essayist,
> *"Of friendship,"* translated by
> Donald M. Frame

"Of all the means to insure happiness throughout the whole of life, by far the most important is the acquisition of friends."

—Epicurus

"Jonathan and Eleanor like each other. They are just eight and ten months old, respectively, which places them at about the youngest ages at which children can display friendship that psychologists can observe and measure."

—Michael Thompson, psychologist, and C. Grace with L. J. Cohen, *Best Friends, Worst Enemies* (2001)

_____

_____

_____

_____

_____

_____

_____

_____

_____

_____

_____

_____

_____

_____

_____

_____

_____

_____

_____

_____

"The more you sincerely listen to your friend, the more your friends are pulled toward you."

—Jan Yager, *Friendshifts*

"*Everyone recognizes friendship, although nobody knows exactly what it is.*
And everyone surely wants to experience it, although friendship cannot be purchased and withers promptly at the hands of those who try to force it to flower."

—Eugene Kennedy, *On Being a Friend* (1982)

"A good friend never gets insulted when you want to be alone."

—Joseph Cohen (*Good Friend*)

"I am worthy of a positive friendship." (Affirmation #1)

—Jan Yager, *365 Daily Affirmations for Friendship*

_____

_____

_____

_____

_____

_____

_____

_____

_____

_____

_____

_____

_____

_____

_____

_____

_____

_____

_____

_____

_____

_____

_____

_____

_____

_____

_____

"A principal fruit of friendship is the ease and discharge of the fullness and swellings of the heart...to whom you may impart griefs, joys, fears, hopes, suspicions, counsels, and whatsoever lieth upon the heart to oppress it, in a kind of civil shrift or confession."

—Sir Francis Bacon, essayist, "Of friendship," The Essays, XXVII (1625)

"The meeting of two personalities is like the contact of two chemical substances; if there is any reaction, both are transformed."

—Carl Jung, psychologist

*"A faithful friend is a
sure shelter,
Whoever finds one has found
a rare treasure."*

—Ecclesiasticus

> *"To me, fair friend, you never can be old,*
> *For as you were when first your eye I eyed,*
> *Such seems your beauty still."*
> —William Shakespeare, *Sonnet 104*

"If you want to win friends, make a point to remember them. If you remember my name, you pay me a subtle compliment. You indicate that I have made an impression on you. Remember my name and you add to my feeling of importance."

—Dale Carnegie, *How to Win Friends and Influence People*

"*Friendship is a very real and close thing. It is one of the greatest joys in life and has noble fruits. We can do much for each other: there are burdens we can share; we can rejoice with those who do rejoice, and weep with those who weep.*"

—Hugh Black, *The Art of Being a Good Friend* (1898)

_____

_____

_____

_____

_____

_____

_____

_____

_____

_____

_____

_____

_____

_____

_____

_____

_____

_____

_____

_____

_____

_____

"That's how it is with people sometimes. When you least expect it, a common thread—golden, at that—begins to weave together the fabric of friendship."

—Mary Kay Shanley, *She Taught me to Eat Artichokes* (1993)

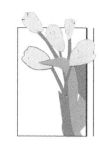

"Of course, there will be some envy or jealousy, as well as competitiveness, in even healthy friendship...What distinguishes a healthy friendship is the level and degree: how much envy, jealousy, or competitiveness occurs, and how often? Is it occasional, or is there a consistent, mean-spirited element to it?"

—Jan Yager, *When Friendship Hurts* (2002)

"I do then with my friends as I do with my books. I would have them where I can find them, but I seldom use them."
—Ralph Waldo Emerson, *"Friendship,"* Essay VI

_____

_____
_____
_____
_____
_____
_____
_____
_____
_____
_____
_____
_____
_____
_____
_____
_____
_____
_____
_____
_____
_____
_____
_____
_____
_____
_____
_____
_____

"If I truly love one person, I love all persons, I love the world, I love life. If I can say to somebody else, 'I love you,' I must be able to say, 'I love you in everybody, I love through you the world, I love in you also myself.'"

—Erich Fromm, *The Art of Loving* (1956)

"The costliness of keeping friends does not lie in what one does for them but in what one, out of consideration for them, refrains from doing."

—Henrik Ibsen, Norwegian playwright

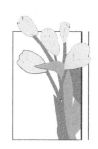

"It is great to have friends when one is young, but indeed it is still greater when one is getting old. When we are young, friends are, like everything else, a matter of course. In the old days we know what it means to have them."

—Edvard Grieg, Norwegian composer

"Love is blind; friendship closes its eyes."
—Anonymous

_____

_____

_____

_____

_____

_____

_____

_____

_____

_____

_____

_____

_____

_____

_____

_____

_____

_____

_____

_____

_____

_____

_____

_____

_____

_____

_____

"Beware of those who attach great value to being credited with moral tact and subtlety in making moral distinctions. They never forgive us once they have made a mistake in front of us (or, worse, against us): inevitably they become our instinctive slanderers and detractors, even if they should still remain our 'friends.' Blessed are the forgetful; for they get over their stupidities, too."

—Friedrich Nietzsche, *Beyond Good and Evil* (1886)

"Girlfriends are those women who know us better than anyone (sometimes better than we know ourselves)."

—Carmen Renee Berry and Tamara Traeder, *Girlfriends: Invisible Bonds, Enduring Ties* (1995)

> *"I had three chairs in my house; one for solitude; two for friendship; three for society."*
>
> —Henry David Thoreau, *Walden* (1854)

"*For when fortune smiles on us, friendship adds a luster to that smile; when she frowns, friendship absorbs her part and share of that frown, and thus makes it easier to bear.*"

—Cicero, "On Friendship," translated by Frank O. Copley

"A man cannot be too careful in the choice of his enemies."

—Oscar Wilde, playwright and novelist,
The Picture of Dorian Gray (1891)

_____

_____

_____

_____

_____

_____

_____

_____

_____

_____

_____

_____

_____

_____

_____

_____

_____

_____

_____

_____

_____

_____

_____

_____

_____

_____

_____

_____

"A close or best friend should stand up for you at work and also act as your extra eyes and ears to deal with office politics...As a young woman who works for a store in Illinois, describing her close friendship with a co-worker in the same department, put it: 'We look out for each other.'"

—Jan Yager, *Who's That Sitting at My Desk?*

"Friends share all things."

—Pythagoras, *Diogenes Laertius, VIII*

"*Make a man laugh a good hearty laugh, and you've paved the way for friendship. When a man laughs with you, he, to some extent, likes you.*"

—Dale Carnegie, *How to Win Friends and Influence People*

> *"Have no friends not equal to yourself."*
> —Confucius (551-479 B.C.), *The Confucian Analects*

"We should exercise such care in making friends that we would never offer affection to someone whom we might someday come to hate."
—Cicero, "On Friendship" Translated by Frank O. Copley

> *"How you and your friend deal with anger in your relationship, when or if it does occur, may be as pivotal a predictor of how dependable your friendship is as how you cope with conflict when and if it arises."*
> —Jan Yager, *When Friendship Hurts*

"Better be a nettle in the side of your friend than his echo."
—Ralph Waldo Emerson, *"Friendship,"* Essay VI

> *"Avoid misusing friends as therapists, nurses, or banks. "*
> —Jan Yager, *Friendshifts* (1999)

"The good befriend themselves."

—Sophocles (c. 495-406 B.C.), *Oedipus at Colonus*

"A betrayer of secrets forfeits
all esteem and will never
find the kind of friend
he wants.
Be fond of a friend and keep
faith with him, but if you
have betrayed his secrets, do
not pursue him any more;
For as a many destroy
his enemy, so you have
destroyed the friendship of
your neighbor..."

—Ecclesiasticus

_____

_____

_____

_____

_____

_____

_____

_____

_____

_____

_____

_____

_____

_____

_____

_____

_____

_____

_____

_____

_____

What could be finer than to have someone to whom you may speak as freely as to yourself?"

—Cicero, *"On Friendship,"* translated by Frank O. Copley

_____

_____

_____

_____

_____

_____

_____

_____

_____

_____

_____

_____

_____

_____

_____

_____

_____

_____

_____

_____

_____

_____

_____

_____

_____

_____

_____

_____

"Lend your money and lose your friend."

—Proverb

"Friends have all things in common."
—Plato (c. 428-348 B.C.), *Dialogues, Phaedrus*

"What is a friend? A single soul dwelling in two bodies."
—Aristotle (384-322 B.C.), *Diogenes Laertius, Lives of Eminent Philosophers, Book V, Section 20*

"My best friend is the one who brings out the best in me."
—Henry Ford

_____

_____

_____

_____

_____

_____

_____

_____

_____

_____

_____

_____

_____

_____

_____

_____

_____

_____

_____

_____

_____

_____

_____

_____

_____

_____

_____

_____

_____

_____

_____

_____

_____

_____

_____

> *"Even if a friendship is had only briefly, it is a plus."*
>
> —Jennifer Holland, *Unlikely Friendships*

"Writing letters has always been a very real part of my life, especially in the years I have been in the field. For then letters home, letters to colleagues—particularly Ruth Benedict and Geoffrey Gorer—and bulletin letters to a widening circle of family and friends have linked my life to theirs in a way that is fast disappearing from a world in which most people communicate by telephone and, very occasionally, by tape recording."

—anthropologist Margaret Mead,
Blackberry Winter: My Earlier Years (1972)

> *"Just because you and your friends work together does not mean either the business or the friendship are doomed."*

From Strategy #36, *"Sort Out the Challenges of Working With a Friend"*

—Jan Yager, *Productive Relationships*

_____

_____

_____

_____

_____

_____

_____

_____

_____

_____

_____

_____

_____

_____

_____

_____

_____

_____

_____

_____

_____

_____

_____

_____

_____

_____

_____

_____

"One's friends are that part of the human race with which one can be human."

—Santayana

*"Four be the things I am
wiser to know:
Idleness, sorrow, a friend,
and a foe."*
—Dorothy Parker, *Enough Rope* (1927)

"Success in many careers is based on relationship building, and nothing builds a trusting relationship faster than the elusive and magical relationship known as friendship".

—Jan Yager, *Friendshifts*

"We must be our own before we can be another's."
—Ralph Waldo Emerson,
"Friendship," Essay VI

"No act of kindness, no matter how small, is ever wasted."

—Aesop (c. 580 B.C.), *The Lion and the Mouse*, quoted in *Bartlett's Familiar Quotations*, from translation by R.D. Hicks

*"The best of friends
must part."*

—Proverb

"I desire so to conduct the affairs of this administration that if at the end, when I come to lay down the reins of power, I have lost every other friend on earth, I shall at least have one friend left, and that friend shall be down inside me."

—Abraham Lincoln (1809-1865), U.S. president, *Reply to the Missouri Committee of Seventy (1864)*

> *"I rejoice in others' successes,*
> *knowing that there is plenty*
> *for us all."*

—Louise L. Hay, #45, *Power Thoughts: 365 Daily Affirmations*

"No road is long with good company."
—Turkish proverb

"A Father's a Treasure;
a Brother's a Comfort;
a Friend is both."
—Benjamin Franklin,
Poor Richard's Almanac

"Now friendship is just this and nothing else: complete sympathy in all matters of importance, plus goodwill and affection."

—Cicero, *"On Friendship,"* translated by Frank O. Copley

"Friendship is always a sweet responsibility, never an opportunity."
—Kahil Gibran

"Deep friendships often result in knowing, frequently without asking, what the other feels and needs."

—Carmen Renee Berry and Tamara Traeder, *Girlfriends: Invisible Bonds, Enduring Ties* (1995)

No man is an island,
Entire of itself,
Every man is a piece of
the continent,
A part of the main.
If a clod be washed away
by the sea,
Europe is the less.
As well as if a promontory were.
As well as if a manor of
thy friend's
Or of thine own were:
Any man's death diminishes me,
Because I am involved
in mankind,
And therefore never send to know
for whom the bell tolls;
It tolls for thee.

—John Donne, English poet (1572-1631)

"Save us from our friends."
—Proverb

"I still must seek the friend
Who does with nature blend,
Who is the person in
her mask,
He is the man I ask."

—Henry David Thoreau, "Great Friend"

"There are friendships based on passion, on pity, on pleasure, on companionship, on professional advantage, on camaraderie-in-arms, on intellectual agreement, on mutual admiration, on spiritual conviction, on personal advancement, on hero worship, on protection, on fear, on need, on loyalty...That all friendships, both personal and national, have in common is that they are voluntary."

—Roger Rosenblatt, "Friends and Countrymen," Time, July 21, 1980

"Although the wish to become, and remain, friends must be shared by both acquaintances, what you share need not be equal."

—Jan Yager, *Friendshifts*

"The secret of friendship is just the secret of all spiritual blessing. The way to get is to give. In the end, the selfish can never get anything but selfishness. The hard find hardness everywhere. As you mete, it is meted out to you."
—Hugh Black, *The Art of Being a Good Friend* (1898)

"If you have drawn your sword on a friend, do not despair; there is a way back.
If you have opened your mouth against your friend, do not worry; there is hope for reconciliation;
But insult, arrogance, betrayal of secrets, and the stab in the back—
in these cases any friend will run away."

—Ecclesiasticus

"Friendship with oneself is all important because without it one cannot be friends with anyone in the world."

—First Lady Eleanor Roosevelt

"Be slow in choosing your friends; slower in changing."

—Benjamin Franklin

"Friendship matters to women; it matters a lot; women today—with lives often in transition—depend on friendship more than ever."

—Ellen Goodman and Patricia O'Brien,
I Know Just What You Mean

"I embrace travel as an opportunity to reconnect with old friends and to meet new ones." (Affirmation #365)

—Jan Yager, *365 Daily Affirmations for Friendship* (2012)

_____
_____
_____
_____
_____
_____
_____
_____
_____
_____
_____
_____
_____
_____
_____
_____
_____
_____
_____
_____
_____
_____
_____
_____

"The only reward of virtue is virtue, the only way to have a friend is to be one."
—Ralph Waldo Emerson,
"Friendship," Essay VI

"Suzanne de Passe Le Mat, an executive at Motown, is my best friend. We've been close ever since we were little girls. Whenever I'm carrying on about how I didn't go to college and how different life could have been if I had, she gets me right back to reality. Tracy Suzanne, my daughter, is named for her."
—singer Diana Ross, quoted in Zivs Kwitney's article, "Bosom Buddies," in the *Seattle Post-Intelligencer* (2/15/81)

_____

_____

_____

_____

_____

_____

_____

_____

_____

_____

_____

_____

_____

_____

_____

_____

_____

_____

"Even the death of friends will inspire us as much as their lives....Their memories will be encrusted over with sublime and pleasing thoughts, as monuments of other men are overgrown with moss; for our friends have no place in the graveyard."

—Henry David Thoreau, *A Week on the Concord and Merrimack Rivers* (1849)

"*Do you know the most important trait a man can have? It is not executive ability; it is not a great mentality; it is not kindliness, nor courage, nor a sense of humor, though each of these is of tremendous importance. In my opinion, it is the ability to make friends, which, boiled down, means the ability to see the best in man.*"

—Dale Carnegie, *How to Win Friends and Influence People*

"In the end we will not remember the words of our enemies, but the silence of our friends."

—Martin Luther King

"In isolation—whether real or emotional—we lose perspective on life."

—Kathleen Brehony, Ph.D., clinical psychologist (Living a Connected Life) (2003)

"*The highest and finest of all human relationships is, arguable, friendship. Consider the fact that we regard it as a success if we become friends with our parents when we grow up, our children when they grow up, our classmates or workmates even as they remain classmates or workmates, for in every such case an additional bond comes to exist, which transcends the other reasons we entered into association with those people in the first place.*"

—A C Grayling, *Friendship* (2013)

More Friendship Quotes

Use the space below to fill in other quotes about friendship that you find or that you compose that you want to add to *Friendship Thoughts, Famous Quotes, and a Journal.*

More Friendship Quotes

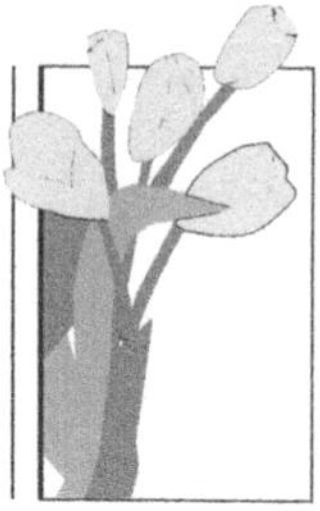

More Friendship Quotes

Use these blank pages to create your own drawings or to post pictures of your friends.

Friendship Self-quiz*

Consider asking yourself these eight questions about your close or best friendships to assess the current quality of the friendship:

1. Do you and your friend communicate -- by phone, fax, letters, or e-mail -- or get together as often as you and your friend want to?
2. Do you and your friend have fun together?
3. When you and your friend speak on the phone, or get together, do you feel connected and appreciated by your friend?
4. Is this friendship basically reciprocal (rather than one way)?
5. Do you and your friend share the same values on issues that matter to you both or, if you do not, are these value disparities easily overlooked?
6. Do you like this friend?
7. Has this friendship stood the test of time and structural changes such as graduating, moving, getting married, switching jobs, or having children?
8. Is conflict with this friend minimal or, if it does occur, are you able to resolve it without long-term resentment?

If you answered "no" to one or more of the above questions about a particular friendship, it may indicate that you or your friend need to do some work on your relationship.

*Excerpted, with permission, from Friendshifts®: The Power of Friendship and How It Shapes Our Lives by Dr. Jan Yager (Hannacroix Creek Books, www.Hannacroixcreekbooks.com)

Finding Time for Friends

Here are some ways to keep up with your friends, no matter how busy you are*:

1. Keep postcards with you so if you have a spare moment while waiting in the doctor's office, sitting around while your child is taking guitar lessons or playing soccer, while commuting, or away on a business trip, so you can use those moments to write to your friends, especially your out-of-town friends, bringing them up to date on your news and keeping in contact.

2. Consider having a holiday celebration for just friends the day after Thanksgiving if you spend Thanksgiving with your relatives. Take turns alternating what friend is responsible for the food or have everyone bring along a dish or beverage. Include the same friends each year or invite different friends from year-to-year.

3. Plan to meet at the neighborhood supermarket or drive together, or meet, and shop together at a local or far away store or mall.

4. Have the phone numbers, addresses, E-mail addresses, and schedules of your friends handy so you can easily call or send a note or E-mail whenever you want to.

5. Make a commitment to get together on a regular basis, depending upon time and distance, on your own or with your spouses or families.

6. Remember your friend's birthday by calling, sending a card, or getting together. Here are a few gift ideas: a picture frame; a book; a journal; or a store or restaurant gift certificate.

7. Volunteer to work in a soup kitchen, tutor children, spend time with the elderly in assisted living communities, read to elementary school children, or tutor together with your friend.

*Excerpted, with permission, from the 31 ways to keep up with your friends from Friendshifts®: The Power of Friendship and How It Shapes Our Lives by Dr. Jan Yager (Hannacroix Creek Books, 2nd edition).

A Checklist for a Positive Friendship*

☐ You like (or love) each other.

☐ You have fun together.

☐ You share confidences, activities, talking, and/or emotional support.

☐ Trust, honesty, and loyalty are expected.

☐ There is little or no jealousy.

☐ Competitiveness is minimal and healthy.

☐ Contact is as frequent as both need and want.

☐ Confidences are kept.

☐ Gossip is non-existent or extremely rare.

☐ Friends are not used or put in compromising positions.

☐ Promises are kept.

☐ Borrowed items are returned.

☐ Tact is practiced.

☐ Honesty is essential but not misused for hurtful reasons.

☐ The friendship is flexible, changing as situations or needs change, or shift for one or both friends because of school, career, or personal reasons.

☐ No matter how busy each friend gets, the friendship is still a priority concern.

☐ Each friend is there for the other, in fair or foul weather.

☐ You have a lot in common but enough that is different to make the relationship interesting.

☐ The relationship is equal.

*Excerpted from Chapter 2, *When Friendship Hurts: How to Deal With Friends Who Betray, Abandon or Wound You* by Jan Yager, Ph.D. (Simon & Schuster, Inc.,/Touchstone, 2002; audio version, Brilliance Audio, 2012.)

Friendship Oath*

By Dr. Jan Yager

By accepting the responsibility of friendship, I promise to be honest and trustworthy. I will try to work out any conflicts that we may have and will try to put the time and effort into our friendship that it requires.

I know we both have work (or school), family, and personal obligations, and we will respect each other's other relationships and commitments, but I will also be committed to this friendship. I will try to only give advice if you ask for it, unless, in my best judgment, I should volunteer it. I will also try to always be your friend, unconditionally.

I will keep your confidences. However, I will also share with you if it is my policy to never keep anything form my spouse or any other primary relationship, with whom I entrust all my secrets. I will try to remember your birthday and be there for you when times are tough and when times are grand.

Making time to talk, communicating by mail or e-mail, or getting together is a priority. I will celebrate your achievements even though I know a tiny bit of envy or competitiveness is normal. I will bring fun and joy to your life as much as I am able to as I cherish our past, present, and future friendship.

Contact Information

Yes, you may already have this information in your smart phone, computer, or paper phone book, but it could be helpful to have information about your key friends here if your phone loses its battery power or you just want to include it right here in this quote book and journal. If you need more pages, photocopy a blank page before filling it in with details.

Name

Address

Cell Phone

Other Phone

E-mail

Facebook Address

LinkedIn Address

Twitter Name

Notes

Name

Address

Cell Phone

Other Phone

E-mail

Facebook Address

LinkedIn Address

Twitter Name

Notes

Name _____

Address _____

Cell Phone _____

Other Phone _____

E-mail _____

Facebook Address _____

LinkedIn Address _____

Twitter Name _____

Notes _____

Name _____

Address _____

Cell Phone _____

Other Phone _____

E-mail _____

Facebook Address _____

LinkedIn Address _____

Twitter Name _____

Notes _____

Name _____

Address _____

Cell Phone _____

Other Phone _____

E-mail _____

Facebook Address _____

LinkedIn Address _____

Twitter Name _____

Notes _____

Name _____

Address _____

Cell Phone _____

Other Phone _____

E-mail _____

Facebook Address _____

LinkedIn Address _____

Twitter Name _____

Notes _____

Name _____

Address _____

Cell Phone _____

Other Phone _____

E-mail _____

Facebook Address _____

LinkedIn Address _____

Twitter Name _____

Notes _____

Name _____

Address _____

Cell Phone _____

Other Phone _____

E-mail _____

Facebook Address _____

LinkedIn Address _____

Twitter Name _____

Notes _____

Name _____

Address _____

Cell Phone _____

Other Phone _____

E-mail _____

Facebook Address _____

LinkedIn Address _____

Twitter Name _____

Notes _____

Name _____

Address _____

Cell Phone _____

Other Phone _____

E-mail _____

Facebook Address _____

LinkedIn Address _____

Twitter Name _____

Notes _____

Name _____

Address _____

Cell Phone _____

Other Phone _____

E-mail _____

Facebook Address _____

LinkedIn Address _____

Twitter Name _____

Notes _____

Name _____

Address _____

Cell Phone _____

Other Phone _____

E-mail _____

Facebook Address _____

LinkedIn Address _____

Twitter Name _____

Notes _____

Name _____

Address _____

Cell Phone _____

Other Phone _____

E-mail _____

Facebook Address _____

LinkedIn Address _____

Twitter Name _____

Notes _____

Name _____

Address _____

Cell Phone _____

Other Phone _____

E-mail _____

Facebook Address _____

LinkedIn Address _____

Twitter Name _____

Notes _____

Name _____

Address _____

Cell Phone _____

Other Phone _____

E-mail _____

Facebook Address _____

LinkedIn Address _____

Twitter Name _____

Notes _____

Name _____

Address _____

Cell Phone _____

Other Phone _____

E-mail _____

Facebook Address _____

LinkedIn Address _____

Twitter Name _____

Notes _____

Name _____

Address _____

Cell Phone _____

Other Phone _____

E-mail _____

Facebook Address _____

LinkedIn Address _____

Twitter Name _____

Notes _____

Name _____

Address _____

Cell Phone _____

Other Phone _____

E-mail _____

Facebook Address _____

LinkedIn Address _____

Twitter Name _____

Notes _____

Name _____

Address _____

Cell Phone _____

Other Phone _____

E-mail _____

Facebook Address _____

LinkedIn Address _____

Twitter Name _____

Notes _____

Name _____

Address _____

Cell Phone _____

Other Phone _____

E-mail _____

Facebook Address _____

LinkedIn Address _____

Twitter Name _____

Notes _____

Name _____

Address _____

Cell Phone _____

Other Phone _____

E-mail _____

Facebook Address _____

LinkedIn Address _____

Twitter Name _____

Notes _____

Name _____

Address _____

Cell Phone _____

Other Phone _____

E-mail _____

Facebook Address _____

LinkedIn Address _____

Twitter Name _____

Notes _____

Name _____

Address _____

Cell Phone _____

Other Phone _____

E-mail _____

Facebook Address _____

LinkedIn Address _____

Twitter Name _____

Notes _____

Resources

www.drjanyager.com
www.whenfriendshiphurts.com

The websites for my books and articles about friendship and information on the annual May International New Friends, Old Friends Week. You will also find videos of my TV appearances about friendship on the *Oprah Winfrey Show*, the *Today Show*, and *Good Morning, America*. Information on upcoming webinars, seminars, or new publications.

A Band of Women
abandofwives.ning.com

A membership networking site for women to connect founded by Christine Bronstein.

www.girlfriendology.com

Founded by Debba Haupert, includes a blog, podcast, and a community for fostering female friendships.

www.thefriendshipblog.com

Blog maintained by psychologist Irene Levine, Ph.D. author of *Best Friends Forever*.

www.friendship.com.au

The Friendship Page, started in 1996 by Australian Bronwyn Polson, includes a friendship chat room, quotes on friendship, as well as highlight the annual International Friendship Day.

www. Executivegirlfriendsgroup.com

EGG, founded by business entrepreneur Chicke Fitzgerald, offers a podcast on friendship-related topics as well as local networking opportunities.

www.girlfriendcircles.com

Founded by Shasta Nelson, a membership friendship networking site to help women connect locally.

www.socialjane.com

Founded by Janis Kupferer, Social Jane is a networking site for finding female friends; membership dues are a one-time fee of $14.95.

www.selfgrowth.com

Free online resource with articles and videos on friendship and other relationship topics.

whatfriendsdo.com

Founded by Aimee Kandrac and her mother Fran, this free site is an outgrowth of a site that had been developed to coordinate information and help for her sister Stephanie's best friend Laura, who was being treated for a terminal brain tumor. The site helps thousands of friends to work out a way to better help a friend in need.

www.Facebook.com

This free site is usually more of a resource for keeping up with the friends you already have, through sharing of status updates, comments, and photos. However, there are certainly countless examples of new friendships that started on Facebook. (As with all social media, post information about yourself and your loved ones with care.)

www.LinkedIn.com

Popular free social media networking site for business friendships and relationships.

Selected Bibliography

Adler, Alfred. *What Life Could Mean to You*. NY: Putnam's, 1958.

Apter, Terri, et al. *Best Friends: The Pleasures and Perils of Girls' and Women's Friendships*. NY: Crown, 1998.

Aristotle, *Aristotle in Twenty-Three Volumes/Vol. 1, The Nicomachean Ethics*. Translated by H. Rackham. Books 8 & 9. Cambridge, MA: Harvard University Press, 1968.

Bacon, Sir Francis. *"Of Friendship"* (1625), in *Classic Essays in English*, Josephine Mile, ed. Boston: Little, Brown, 1965.

Barkas, J. L. (Janet Lee). *See also* Yager, Jan.

Barkas, J. L. *Friendship: A Selected, Annotated Bibliography*, NY: Garland, 1985.

Baron, Gerald R. *Friendship Marketing*. Grants Pass, OR: Oasis press, PSI Research, 1997.

Cartlett, John. *Bartlett's Familiar Quotations*. 16th edition. Boston: Little, Brown and Company, 1992.

Bernikow, Louise. *Among Women*. NY: Harper and Row, 1980.

Berrey, Carmen Renee and Tamara Traeder, *Girlfriends*. Berkeley, CA: Wildcat Canyon Press, 1995.

Black, Hugh. *The Art of Being a Good Friend*. Manchester, NH: Sophia Institute Press, 1999 (1898).

Bronstein, Christine and A Band of Wives. *Nothing But the Truth So Help Me God: 51 Women Reveal the Power of Positive Female Connections*. Nothing But the Truth, LLC, 2012.

Carnegie, Dale. *How to Win Friends and Influence People*. NY: Pocket Books, 1940 (1936).

Cicero. *On Old Age and on Friendship.* Translated by Frank O. Copley. Anne Arbor: University of Michigan Press, 1967.

Cohen, Joseph. *A Good Friend.* Illustrations by Debra Solomon. NY: Workman Publishing, 1986.

Cott, Nancy. *The Bonds of Womanhood.* New Haven, CT: Yale University Press, 1977.

Davis, Bette. *The Lonely Life.* NY: Putnam, 1961.

Degler, Carl N. *At Odds: Women and the Family in America from the Revolution to the Present.* NY: Oxford University Press, 1980.

Elman, Natalie Madorsky and Eileen Kennedy-Moore. *The Unwritten Rules of Friendship*. NY: Little, Brown, 2003.

Emerson, Ralph Waldo. *"Friendship,"* in *Essays by Ralph Waldo Emerson*, NY: Harper and Row. 1951, pp. 121–156.

Enright, D.J., and David Rawlinson, eds. *The Oxford Book of Friendship*. NY: Oxford University Press, 1992.

Fromm, Erich. *The Art of Loving*. NY: Harper, 1956.

Gabor, Don. *How to Start a Conversation and Make Friends*. NY: Simon and Schuster (Fireside), 1983.

Goodman, Ellen, and Patricia O'Brien. *I Know Just What You Mean*. NY: Simon and Schuster, 2000.

Grayling, A.C. *Friendship*. New Haven, CT: Yale University Press, 2013.

Green, Deborah Chenault. *Back 2/1: I Invite You Into My Serenity: A Collection of Poetry and Prose*. Bloomington, IN: iUniverse, 2008.

Greive, Bradley Trevor. *Friends to the End*. Kansas City, KS: Andrews McMeel Publishing, LLC, 2004.

Haupert, Debba and Girfriendology.com. *Girlfriendology 101*. Girlfriendology LLC, 2011.

Holland, Jennifer. *Unlikely Friendships*. NY: Workman, 2011.

James, Muriel and L. M. Savary. *The Heart of Friendship*. NY: Harper, 1976.

Klam, Julie. *Friendkeeping*. NY: Riverhead Books (Penguin), 2012.

Knowles, Elizabeth, ed. *The Oxford Dictionary of Quotations. Oxford*, UK: Oxford University Press, 5th ed, 1999.

Lazarsfeld, Paul F., and Robert K. Merton. *"Friendship as Social Process: A Substantive and Methodological Analysis,"* in *Freedom and Control in Modern Society*, M. Berger, T. Abel, and C. Page, eds. NY: Van Nostrand, 1954, pp. 18–66.

Levine, Irene S. *Best Friends Forever*. NY: Overlook Press, 2009.

Matousek, Mark. *Ethical Wisdom for Friends*. Deerfield Beach, FL: 2013.

McGinnis, Alan Joy. *The Friendship Factor*. Minn, MN: Augsburg Fortress, 2004; 1979.

Mead, Margaret. *Blackberry Winter.* NY: Morrow, 1972.

Montaigne. *"Of Friendship,"* in *The Complete Essays of Montaigne,* translated by Donald M. Frame. Stanford, CA: Stanford University Press, 1958, pp. 135–144.

Nelson, Shasta. *Friendships Don't Just Happen!* Nashville, TN: Turner Publishing, 2013.

Plato, Lysis, or Friendship in *The Works of Plato.* Translated by Jowett. NY: Modern Library, 1956.

Pogrebin, Letty Cottin. *Among Friends.* NY: McGraw Hill, 1985.

Purcell, Maud. *"The Health Benefits of Journaling."* www.psychcentral.com/lib/2006/the-health-benefits-of-journaling

Shain, Merle. *When Lovers are Friends.* Philadelphia, PA: Lippincott, 1978.

Shanley, Mary Kay. *She Taught Me to Eat Artichokes.* Marshalltown, IA: Sta-Kris, Inc., 1993.

Smedes, Lewis. *The Art of Forgiving.* NY: Ballantine, 1997.

Smyth, J. M.; A. Stone; A. Hurewitz; and A.Kaell. *"Effects of Writing about Stressful Experiences on Symptom Reduction in Patients with Asthma or Rheumatoid Arthritis."* JAMA, April 14, 1999, Vol. 281, No. 14, pages 1304-1309.

Spencer, Liz and Ray Pahl. *Rethinking Friendship: Hidden Solidarities Today.* Princeton, NJ: Princeton U Press, 2006.

Taylor, Irene and Alan Taylor. *The Assassin's Cloak: An Anthology of the World's Greatest Diarists.* Edinburgh, UK: Canongate UK, 2000.

Thoreau, Henry David, *Portable Thoreau,* NY: Viking, 1964.

University of Rochester, *"Journaling for Mental Health,"* *URHE* (University of Rochester Health Encyclopedia.) http://www.urmc.rochester.edu/encyclopedia/content.aspx?Cont entTypeID=1&ContentID=4552

Vernon, Mark. *The Philosophy of Friendship.* NY: Palgrave Macmillan, 2005.

Welty, Eudora and Ronald A. Sharp, editors. *The Norton Book of Friendship.* NY: Norton, 1991.

Whelchel, Lisa. *Friendship for Grown-ups.* Nashville, TN: Thomas Nelson, 2010.

Yager, Jan. *365 Daily Affirmations for Friendship.* Stamford, CT: Hannacroix Creek Books, Inc., 2012.

_____. *Friendshifts®: The Power of Friendship and How It Shapes Our Lives.* Stamford, CT: Hannacroix Creek Books, 1997, 2nd edition 1999; updated e-book and audiobook editions, 2013.

_____. *"Perspectives on Friendship."* Ray Kirshak, editor, *International Journal of Sociology and Social Policy.* Vol. 18, No. 1, 1998, pp. 27–40.

_____.*When Friendship Hurts.* NY: Simon & Schuster/Touchstone, 2002, Brilliance Audio, 2012.

About Jan Yager

Dr. Jan Yager, who is a friendship coach as well as a workshop leader and speaker, has been studying friendship since it was the topic of her sociology dissertation. Her books on friendship and relationships, include: *When Friendship Hurts; Friendshifts; 365 Daily Affirmations for Friendship; 365 Daily Affirmations for Happiness; Who's That Sitting at My Desk?; Productive Relationships; Business Protocol;* and *125 Ways to Meet the Love of Your Life.*

For more on this author/expert/coach/artist,/speaker, visit her websites which includes media clips and original blogs:
http://www.drjanyager.com *or*
http://www.whenfriendshiphurts.com

Follow her tweets at: www.twitter.com/drjanyager

Visit the publishing company she founded in 1996, Hannacroix Creek Books: http://www.hannacroixcreekbooks.com

Follow their tweets at: http://www.twitter.com/hannacroixcreek

To book Jan for a workshop or speech, contact your favorite speaker bureau or Jan directly at: yagerinquiries2@aol.com.

Other journals by Jan Yager that you might find of interest
Available wherever books are sold or directly from the publisher
www.hannacroixcreekbooks.com
hannacroix@aol.com

ISBN: 978-1-889262-79-6 (hardcover)
ISBN: 978-1-889262-80-2 (trade paperback)

Birthday Tracker and Journal is a special place to record important birthdays for family, friends, and others, month by month. It includes an informative introduction on birthday celebration traditions and lists birthday birthstones and flowers by month for gift-giving considerations. There is also a place to keep track of birthday cards or presents that you send, or receive, lined blank pages for your birthday reflections, and a place for birthday photos. Color illustrations by author/artist Jan Yager appear throughout. This unique book is a perfect gift or for one's own use to organize this special birthday information.

Praise for Birthday Tracker and Journal:

"Yager's *Birthday Tracker* helps me stay organized not only with the months but also has plenty of pages for notes and photos. I also love her introduction of the history of birthday celebrations and traditions. Keep the *Birthday Tracker & Journal* permanently on your desk so you can be looking forward to the next celebration. I promise it will keep a smile on your face."
—*Beverly Solomon, business manager for artist Pablo Solomon*

Made in the USA
Middletown, DE
11 September 2020